THE IMAGE
OF SUCCESS

How to influence, persuade and
perfect your personal presentation

Silvana Patrick

A catalogue record for this book is available from the National Library of Australia

Contents

Preface

I have always loved fashion. As a little girl, I used to dress up my dolls and draw dresses. One of the earliest memories that I recall is asking my mother to buy me "red panties."

People have always turned to me for advice on how to dress for special occasions. I used to read a lot of magazines, particularly Italian, French, and British editions, and soaked up all the information I came across. As I grew up in the 1980s, with all the glamour of the supermodels, I used to read all about the top fashion designers' lives, their creative process, and their brands.

When I love something, I go into it; that's my nature. That was exactly what happened with colour. It started with the red panties and developed into a 'red obsession'. I developed a pattern, becoming so interested in a particular colour that I would have to buy everything in that hue. Then I would move on to another colour, and then another. These phases sparked my curiosity in colour; why was I so drawn to it? I researched everything I could about the subject, including the science behind it and its psychological effect. I taught what I learnt in workshops and will now share it with you in this book.

As you can already tell, when it came to further my education, a fashion degree was the natural path for me. That doesn't mean it would be easy though (something I soon realised). Back when fashion was much more limited and inaccessible than it is today, it was really difficult to break through, especially in my home country of Brazil. I was from a worker's family and none of my relatives had the slightest inclination for fashion. But, despite the barriers I faced, I got a job at a large textile company owned by a traditional Italian family.

I worked hard and learnt so much! It was an incredible experience, and they liked my work. The owners of the factory were the parents of the editor-in-chief of a luxury magazine, so one day I gathered my courage and asked for an opportunity at the magazine. I got it.

The work at the magazine was completely different to the work I was doing before. While I learnt different facets of the business, there wasn't much creativity involved in the early stages. I started to feel I needed other, bigger challenges. I wanted the sky, so when an opportunity to apply for an internship in New York came up, I went for it. And guess what? Yes, I got it.

Soon I was in 'The Big Apple', working for a huge luxury magazine and I couldn't have been more thrilled. The city and the job were a dream come true... or so I thought. The work was hard and not at all glamorous. I carried clothes from floor to floor and dealt with models who were often moody, grumpy, and rude, especially the top ones. Of course, I expected to work hard, but what I didn't appreciate was the fact that I wasn't exercising my creativity. Above all I hated the dynamics of the industry, in particular the competitiveness and the lack of friendship. I didn't share those values and that was difficult.

I tried for as long as I could, but eventually had to give up on my dream of being a fashion designer and find something that would sustain me. It was pretty devastating. It took me a couple of years to come up with something I had some interest in, as all I could think of was fashion. This was almost 25 years ago, when there were few personal stylists around. That kind of thing was for celebrities.

I decided to go back to university and start something new. I earned a degree in Business Administration, followed by an internship. Entering the corporate world was a difficult period of my life. I felt lost and didn't know which way to go, but in the end, I built a successful career for myself. It was hard to transition from my dream of being a fashion designer into a businesswoman. I had to recreate myself by changing the way I dressed and behaved as well. This took time, self-awareness, and I made plenty of mistakes.

In the early days I didn't have a clue how to portray a corporate image. I didn't even want to. I still dressed like a young stylist but that didn't work at all. I had no one to guide me. Nobody will ever tell you that what you are wearing is inappropriate, they will simply close the door. It took several years for me to realise what I was doing, but when I did, I changed it. My career took off. I learnt what it takes to look successful and then I *became* successful.

That personal experience is one I pass on to my clients and students today, and I'm so grateful I can. I worked in the corporate world for 15 years, and experienced lots of ups and downs. Don't get me wrong, I wasn't completely miserable. My career took me to wonderful places and brought me money, but at the end of the day, it was not my passion.

I entered the corporate world mostly because I spoke fluent English, which was a huge advantage back in my hometown. The company I worked for transferred me to the United States, to develop the trade lane between North and South America. I got to know the United States very well and became the US Trade Lane Manager 'Queen'. After a year the company needed someone with my kind of expertise in Melbourne, Australia. So off to Australia I went.

I spent a wonderful, whirlwind year 'down under,' but it was short-lived as I was once again transferred. This time to

Auckland, New Zealand. At that point I started to become a bit frustrated with moving but decided to embrace this new beginning one more time. When I arrived in New Zealand, it was love at first sight. It was so beautiful and laid back and worlds apart from the chaotic lifestyle of the big cities I had lived in before, like Sao Paulo, New York, and Melbourne. In contrast, Auckland felt like a breeze. It was exactly what I needed at that point in my life. I thought to myself, "This is the place I want to live for the rest of my life."

I managed to stay in New Zealand for four years and got promoted to Sales Manager. While I really enjoyed it, fashion was always in the back of my mind. I could not get past the fact that I was not working on my passion after all these years. Yet, I hadn't put any energy into making a change. I carried on doing the same thing, let go of my dream, accepted life as it was and made peace with it.

When I was at my most relaxed and peaceful, I met my husband. It all seemed to be falling into place. Life was good. I was in love, then I fell pregnant and that changed everything, yet again. It became clear that I needed to pursue my passion, and this was the right time. I had been thinking about it for quite some time but didn't have the courage to act. My pregnancy gave me the strength I needed to make a change for my baby, so I could be a good example for her. I felt empowered, so I quit my job and started my consulting agency.

It's been 10 years now and I have no regrets. But the transitions didn't stop there: not only did I become a mother and change careers, but we moved again. Yes, my husband got a job in Doha, Qatar. We decided to embrace the change once more and moved to the Middle East.

We spent nearly four years in Doha. Having moved so many times before, I thought another move was going to be smooth, only to realise it was the most challenging thing I have ever faced in my life. My experience in a Muslim country is a chapter apart, but in sum, it was difficult to adapt to the culture, the weather and the way they do business. Having to learn everything from scratch and not knowing where to start can be quite stressful, particularly to a woman who is used to being independent.

But I gained a lot from that experience. I developed important skills, started public speaking and offering workshops to the expat community, helping them transition into Muslim culture through their clothes. That was extremely beneficial for me.

But after four years it was time to move on again. My husband got a job in Australia, and we embraced it. It was not Melbourne, my preferred city, but we moved anyway, not knowing what we were going to find there. I started my business for the third time from scratch, in a place where I didn't know anyone.

Again, it was a difficult transition, back into the 'real world' after having lived in a surreal place. I brought myself to new challenges and environments. Having worked in the corporate world, combined with all the multicultural exposure and the ability to recreate myself every single time, provided me with all the tools I required to help professionals become successful.

Portraying a successful image brings the success you want, provided that you are good at what you do, of course. And it's measurable. Throughout the years, I have helped many professionals get where they wanted to be, and it's all here in this book. Fifteen years of experience, my eye and my passion for fashion.

I have worked with hundreds of people and lived in several countries, but writing a book comes from a desire to reach a larger audience with my message. It is my contribution to the world to help people become more aware and to encourage them to pursue their dreams. I hope this book inspires you to go out there and get out of your comfort zone, to try new things and see the results for yourself. But the bottom line is, get to know yourself better. Know what your essence is and make it shine.

Chapter 1

The Image of Success

If you look at successful people, you will notice that all of them have something in common: confidence. It shows, it transcends the computer screen, TV and phone. If you ever have the opportunity to meet such a person, you will feel their positive energy. Regardless of whether you like their style, you still know they are successful. There is cohesiveness to their look; the final result is harmonious. Everything makes sense.

Successful people believe they are successful and transfer that belief to all facets of their lives. They use symbols to show and maintain their success. One of the most important aspects of their success is that they often leave nothing to chance. They pay attention to all four aspects of visual image, which includes how they present themselves through clothing, grooming, body language, and manners. In this book, we will explore the clothing aspect of visual image.

The way we dress plays an important role in achieving success because it influences how we feel about ourselves as well as how we feel about others. And, of course, because we need to dress ourselves every day, we need to pay attention to our image and what messages we are portraying. So powerful is the notion of our image and our perception of self that several studies have been published (e.g., Slepian et al., 2015; Kraus & Mendes, 2014) demonstrating that our dress can have a strong effect on others' perceptions of us and of our personal psychological states.

Embodied cognition is an emerging but somewhat controversial field of cognitive science. It was born from the notion that our bodies influence our perceptions and decisions as much as our brains influence our body. As an extension of this theory, Adam and Galinsky (2012) proposed that the clothes we wear can influence the way we feel and even our behaviour. Referring to this as 'enclothed cognition,' they proposed that there is an influence on the symbolic meaning of clothing and related psychological processes. This could moderate a person's behaviour by influencing their actions about the expectations that are created by the felt experience of wearing certain clothing. They also proposed that our perceptions can be subtly influenced by what another person is wearing.

Why Image Matters

Humans are judgmental creatures. We judge everything we lay our eyes on. With time, these judgments become filters. Our judgments stem from past experiences, values, cultural background, and personal preferences. This causes us to compare what is in front of us with our prior lived experiences. It all happens in a matter of seconds. On the flip side, this means we are judged exactly the same way. Most people are not aware of this process, as it is mostly unconscious and seldom discussed amongst others. We may feel that we don't have control over how people perceive us until we know ourselves enough to have influence over this process. This is what this book is about. When we learn exactly what makes us feel a certain way, i.e., confident, and powerful, we can use the impression we give others to influence how others perceive us.

To illustrate my point, take this example: if you had two wrapped gifts in front of you, one beautifully wrapped and one poorly wrapped, and you got to choose between the two without knowing its content, which one would you choose? Chances are, you would pick the beautifully wrapped one! That's because we are drawn to attractive things, and by attractive I do not mean necessarily good looking but rather looking good. There is a difference.

One thing I am sure of, though, is that image matters. I learned this lesson the hard way. In fact, it's safe to say that image matters more today than it ever has before. Human beings are sensitive to images. It is intrinsic in us regardless of whether it's live or virtual. Due to the increase in popularity because of social media, its importance has grown exponentially. I am not saying this with any pretension. To understand the human psyche, I leave it to great people who have studied human psychology. I say this as an image consultant who has vast experience with people and has worked closely enough with them to see the pattern. I have worked with very smart people who were not getting anywhere. In fact, I saw them falling, or worse, not even being given the opportunity to show their skills, because they didn't portray an image that conveyed respect, professionalism, capability, and self-confidence. They were stuck and petrified. That's what fear does to us: it stops us from seeing clearly and taking action. Throughout the years I've heard bosses saying they cannot promote their smartest employees because their image does not correspond with that of the company.

I have always been passionate about helping people feel confident from the outside in (although it's important to work from the inside out as well) and shed some light on how they want to be perceived and how they want to feel about themselves. Everyone is unique and thus has a signature style that will make them stand out from the crowd. There is nothing worse than being a copy of someone else. No matter how good the copy is, it is never as good as the original. As visual creatures, we judge situations and people very quickly, and often without letting them speak first. It's a scientifically proven fact. We are also very susceptible to criticism. Most of the time, we seek approval.

The question is: how can we use this to our advantage? I believe the answer is enhancing awareness, or more specifically, our self-awareness.

I hear you saying, "What does a stylist have to do with all this?" And I respond "Everything." If you think of all the stylish people you know, either in person or on TV, you might think that their style is effortless. But, in fact, they have done their homework. It could be that they come from stylish parents or quite the opposite, which is the case with me. I came from a family of workers who didn't have any sense of style. I remember in my pre-teenage years asking Mom to change her outfit because I thought what she was wearing was not suitable for her body type and/or the occasion. Anyhow, whether they were born like that or somehow inherited these characteristics, there is a lot of work involved. They have scrutinised a magazine or observed their muses, but either way their style has not come easily. Even if you were lucky enough to be born with a defined style, you still have to have great awareness of yourself, your body type, and what works and doesn't work for you. You can be born with it, but you can also learn the necessary skills. In this book, you will find all the information you need so that you can achieve your style goals, regardless of the current state of your style.

Fashion is a bit like politics, whether you like it or not, it's part of life. Seeing that we are all judged by others and ourselves, we might as well be judged on our own terms.

Our clothes influence our state of mind and our confidence, even if we are not aware of it. Have you ever felt that what you were wearing didn't feel right, or have a sense that you were not dressed appropriately? Or felt too self-conscious when you gained or lost weight and your clothes didn't fit? These feelings drain our confidence and isolate us, because when we feel this way, we don't feel like interacting with people. Have you ever had a wardrobe full of clothes yet nothing to wear? This can set the tone of our day. Imagine how you would feel if you had a clean, organised closet where you could see everything you have. That image would follow you throughout the day, making you feel more relaxed and focused. The opposite is also true! When one of the first things we see in the morning is a cluttered wardrobe, we feel stressed, and this instantly changes our mood. If you can't find anything to wear you can be left feeling demotivated, and worse, end up being dressed inappropriately given the commitments for the day.

When we shop for clothes, we usually do so through our emotions, our childhood experiences, our expectations, and our view of ourselves. I had clients who hated shopping because their mom was hard on them when they went shopping, making it a very difficult experience. Others had a very pleasant experience shopping as children, and as a consequence they overdo it in adulthood to recreate that experience. All these patterns are ingrained in our minds and are projected outwards.

Am I being too analytical? That's because it's all psychological. It's like going to the supermarket hungry. We shop to compensate, to recreate a pleasant experience, or to do something that needs to be done. We shop because we want to feel better, more attractive, because we are happy or sad, things are not going well with our partner, we are worried or anxious, etc. Shopping without awareness only reinforces the pattern. In order to make the right decision when it comes to shopping, we need to know ourselves, know what works for us, and have a plan. We are good at making plans and setting goals for our businesses and work, but we forget that our image also requires planning. We cannot expect it to just happen. At every opportunity we must ask ourselves "How do we want people to perceive us?"

If we don't make a checklist of what we really need, that is also aligned with our budget, we end up buying the wrong items or items that don't go with any other ones that we already have in our wardrobe. Just because it was on sale, or we found it pretty. Women spend, on average, US$125,000 on clothes and accessories throughout their lives. If you think about this, you might realise how much money is wasted on items that won't even get worn or will get worn but won't make you look your best. Think how this money could have been spent on items that would actually help you project an image that would make you look great, confident and successful, and help you get that job, promotion, or even that date you really wanted!

Clothes are our packaging and people are drawn to beautifully wrapped gifts without even knowing what's inside. It's in our nature. I've already said this but it's worth repeating. Without getting your image right, you may lose precious opportunities and sometimes we don't get a second chance. When we make a long-lasting impression, people feel like they want to be associated with us. They want to get to know us better. People believe what they see. And if they *think* you are successful, in their eyes you *are* successful. It's not a question of looking beautiful and sexy, it's a matter of looking and feeling great, and of that showing through. It's working from the outside in, regardless of age, body type, or price tag.

Quality is the second most important thing when choosing a garment. Learning how to recognise quality is a valuable skill because it doesn't necessarily correspond with the price of the item. There are numerous quality pieces that are quite affordable, whereas some designer outfits have no quality whatsoever. Therefore, recognising quality in a garment is crucial. When you can combine styles that work for your body type and lifestyle that have quality, you have learnt the two most important factors in achieving a perfect look at all times. We will look in detail at these two lessons later in the book. But this is actually what this book is all about. Knowing what works for you and how to wear it to each and every occasion, combined with quality perennial classic pieces that will last for many seasons to come, is all you need to achieve an impeccable image at all times. It's not complicated; these are simple ideas that I will share in this book. This book is not a mere styling guide but a guide that will teach you how to achieve an impeccable image by using all the styling tools available, combined with the science behind colours and, ultimately, the power of self-awareness.

One of the things that causes the most confusion is the difference between style and trends. They tend to make fashion sound superficial because of the way they are used. So, let's get some clarity. Every single one of us has style. That's what makes us pick a piece over another one. It is also what makes you judge other people, because we judge based on our personal preferences, values, culture, age, financial status, inner state, etc.

Trend is the offer or suggestion. It is what is available out there at any given time. A stylish person, who was born with it or has learnt the skills, knows which trends work for them, so they become the so-called *trend-setters*. Because they are the pioneers wearing a certain trend that makes them look great and current, you will want to 'copy' them, thus you become a *follower*, a copy, and a copy is never as good as the original. I will elaborate more on trends later.

Chapter 2

Knowing What Works for You

There is no way to learn how to dress without getting a bit technical, and there is more science to it than you can imagine, but it is all totally learnable. Let's get into that here. Knowing what works for your particular body type is the first and most important lesson to learn in order to gain self-awareness. Some people are simply better at knowing what works than others, while others were good when they were younger but lost the 'skill' as they aged. Maybe they had more free time for themselves before starting families or becoming busy professionals. Once one gets older and has children, women, in particular, tend to forget about themselves and focus on family. Juggling careers and family is a daunting task. And with that, they also tend to keep the image of their younger body in their minds, not realising that their body has changed.

Many people gain weight after marriage. They change their lifestyle, they exercise less, and end up eating more. But the changes don't occur very fast. Rather, it is the slow, cumulative addition resulting from our choices and because of this, it takes much longer for us to become aware of and accept the changes (and some never do). We all age and our bodies all change, so it's important to make peace with the mirror and make friends with the person you see in it. If you keep it at a distance, chances are you won't recognise what you see reflected in it, or you will see the image distorted by your own filters when you look at it. This often happens.

I am not saying you should be obsessed with looking in the mirror, but don't be afraid of what it's reflecting, because it's you! But it's better to see yourself consistently instead of only realizing the difference after you put on 10 kilos on the scale.

Everyone is different; we have different body types, and most of this is due to our genetics. There is nothing much we can do about it other than use clothes to create the ideal image based on our body type. Clothes can help us create visual balance, enhance our assets and camouflage our perceived flaws. Balance is what we are aiming for here. The human brain looks for symmetry, and that's the beauty of clothing; through all the elements of style, we can create the look that we are drawn to.

It is also important to remember that the perfect body type changes according to society and culture at the time. In older times, a full feminine figure was considered the epitome of sexiness. Back in the 1980s, thanks to Madonna, muscly women were considered to have the ideal body. Nowadays, what we consider a perfect female body type is a balanced, toned, slightly rounded figure, with the shoulders in line with the hips, combined with a smaller waist, which can be called 'hourglass' body type. For men, it varies from culture to culture. In Western countries, an attractive male figure is a trapezius one and in Asian countries it is more on the petite side. Anyway, the key word here is balance, that I cannot emphasise enough. Balance, balance, balance. To achieve a balanced result, we can make use of elements of style: cuts, fabrics, patterns, colours, and contrast.

Styles

So, no style comes without the acknowledgment of body types. Therefore, the first thing to do is get familiar with yours. Body types don't change radically; you may lose or gain weight but, as I shared earlier, this is mostly due to our genetics. You may become, for example, a 'full' hourglass as opposed to a 'neat' hourglass, or vice-versa. Some women gain weight around their midsection after having a baby and some are not able to lose the extra weight, but overall, their body type remains the same. Most stylists call the 'ideal' female body type 'hourglass' due to its similarity in shape to an hourglass. It means the shoulders are equal in size to the hips (and combined with a smaller waist). Our goal is to achieve this shape through the use of clothes and styling techniques.

Therefore if, for instance, you have wider shoulders and flat hips, which is known as the 'inverted triangle shape', it's best for you to keep your upper body clothing simple (in particular, your shoulders) and leave the details, like pockets and pleats, for your bottom part. The right pieces will help you create the illusion of an ideal body type. That's why I am so passionate about what clothes can do for us. When we use this knowledge to our favour, we can create any result we want. So, let's get started.

Body Types

Hourglass

Hourglass can be neat or full
(as well as all body types)

Main characteristics of the hourglass body shapes are that the shoulders are as wide as the hips, and you have a well-defined waist. Full hourglass types have a large bust and round hip.

Golden Rules

For this particular body type, it is crucial to highlight the waist by wearing cinched dresses and tops. When you accentuate your waist, you look slimmer.

Best Styles

Look for pieces that will follow your curves without being too clingy or too stiff, which will add unnecessary volume.

Tops – any type with waist definition, such as wraps. As for jackets and coats, if you have large hips, choose either cropped or long ones that finish below the hip area. This body type generally has a generous bust, so it's important to keep the upper body as simple as possible. Avoid detailing such as frills around the chest and oversized scarves whenever possible.

Necklines – the ideal necklines are V-neck, round scoop or boat-neck, as these elongate the bust area, making it appear smaller. If you have a large bust, avoid turtlenecks altogether as well as large patterns on your top half.

Skirts – the ideal style for an hourglass figure is the A-line, soft pleats, or full skirt.

Pants – your best bets are straight or wide legs that will flow from the waist. These will help de-emphasise the hip area. Avoid skinny pants, pencil skirts and any style that will be too clingy, as well as details at the bottom, such as pleats, protuberant pockets, frills, any large patterns or prints etc, to avoid adding bulk around the hips.

Fabrics

Choose mid-weight fabrics that will follow your curves, ideally without pleats or pockets. A note on length: the length of a garment should always fall at the smallest part of the body, i.e., just above the knee, or mid-arm. Because this body type has characteristically larger hips, the length of a jacket should fall either right at the waist or past the hip area.

SUPER TIP

THE END OF A GARMENT SHOULD FALL AT THE SMALLEST PART OF THE BODY.

Pear

Many women's body types are pear-shaped, due to our constitution and hormones. This body type is characterized by having round shoulders and larger hips, with waist definition. The areas to be worked on are shoulders and hips: we want to create the illusion of square shoulders and minimize the bottom with straight lines.

Best Styles

To create the appearance of squarer, more structured shoulders, your best bets are jackets with shoulder pads. Alternatively, choose tops with shoulder details such as frills or puffy sleeves.

Tops – Should be cinched at the waist, if you don't have a defined waist, instead they should be slightly loose around the waist and tummy area without being too clingy or too loose. Your Jackets and coats should finish either above or below the widest point of your hips and bottom.

Skirts – Following the same rules for the Hourglass type, best options are an A-line or full skirt.

Pants – When it comes to pants and skirts, these should follow the same rules as the hourglass figure: with little or no details, such as pleats and pockets or big patterns. Mid-size vertical stripes on pants or skirts are fine as they have an elongating, therefore slimming, effect. I highly recommend zippers on the side. Separates are a better option than dresses.

Fabrics

Choose fabrics that give some structure to your top half, like wool and crisper fabrics that add some bulk. Choose lightweight fabrics at the bottom, so the garment follows your natural curves, without adding unnecessary volume. Use contrast to your advantage as well. Meaning darker solid colours at your bottom half and lighter colours at your top half. Remember, you want to balance your figure.

Inverted Triangle

This body type is characterized by having wide shoulders and flat hips, with little waist definition. The areas to be worked on are shoulders and hips: we want to minimize the shoulders' width and create curves in the hip area.

Best Styles

Ideally you should de-emphasize the shoulders by not adding details to it and creating volume at the bottom half.

Tops – Recommendable styles such as halter necks or strapless tops and simple tees. Jackets and coats should finish right at your hips. They also should not be cinched at the waist. Instead, they should be slightly loose around the waist and tummy area without being too tight or too loose.

Skirts – Pencil, box pleats or straight.

Pants – When it comes to pants and skirts, you can be more playful and add details such as pleats and pockets and/or patterns. Horizontal stripes on pants and skirts are fine as they accentuate your bottom, therefore balancing the lack of curves.

Fabrics

Choose fabrics that give some structure to your bottom half, such as wool and crisper fabrics that add some bulk. Choose lightweight fabrics at the top, which will balance your figure.

Apple

The opposite of pear shape, this body type's main characteristics are larger shoulders and narrower hips, with little waist definition. Here we must keep the upper body simple, avoiding any details that will make your shoulders appear even larger.

Best Styles

Tops – Keep it simple with clean lines. Avoid shoulder pads and details at the shoulders. Jackets and coats with straight lines.

Pants and skirts – Here pleats and pockets are allowed. Wide and straight leg pants and skirts are also preferable, with zippers on the side. You should also avoid cinched tops and dresses. Empire dresses and tops with V-necks are great options for this particular body type.

Fabrics

Choose fabrics with a bit of weight to your bottom half and crisper fabrics that add some bulk. Choose lightweight fabrics at the top, so the garment follows your natural curves, without adding unnecessary volume. Remember, you want to balance your figure.

Column or Athletic

As the name suggests, this body type tends to not have curves, so the goal is to create some. We achieve this by choosing styles that cinch in the waist and by adding detailing at the top and bottom parts of the body. This body type can wear volume from the head to toe if your waist is cinched, although it is more recommendable to pick one, i.e., if you opt to wear wide leg pants, pick a top that has little detail to it, like a simple t-shirt or tank top, or even a shirt that is closer to the body. The opposite is also valid, if you choose skinny jeans for example, you can wear an oversized top for balance. Pleats and pockets are perfectly fine, as are as stiff fabrics. Avoid figure-hugging styles, like body-con dresses. Wear a belt whenever you can to create the illusion of a waist. This body type looks great in turtlenecks as they make the bust look bigger.

Best Styles

Tops – You can opt for highlighting your top half by choosing styles with some shoulder detailing to them, such as frills, puff sleeves or shoulder pads. Jackets and coats should be waisted with some details to them such as pockets.

Pants and skirts – In case you opt for highlighting your bottom half, pleats and pockets are your best bets as well as patterns. Remember: the smaller the body frame, the smaller should be the pattern, so if you are more on the petite side, pick small patterns. Wide and straight leg pants and skirts also work well. You should also invest on cinched tops and dresses.

Fabrics

Choose fabrics with a bit of weight to them so they add some volume and don't forget to add a belt or styles that cinch at the waist. Remember, you want to create the illusion of a waist.

Round

Characterized by round shoulders and no waist definition, a round body type needs to focus mostly on the weight of fabrics; they should be lightweight with few patterns. I will go in depth into patterns later. This particular body type needs to avoid unnecessary volume in both the top and bottom parts of their body, so no pleats, frills, or pockets should be worn.

Best Styles

Tops – Opt for shawls or wide-shaped tops that cascade down the body, you can also choose jackets with a small shoulder pad to create some structure at the shoulders and V-neckline. Cardigans are a great option.

Pants and skirts – These should be adjustable at the waist for more comfort; wraps and flip skirts are great as well as wide leg pants. Choose those with zippers on the side to minimize volume.

Fabrics

Choose from light to mid-weight fabrics that are pliable enough to follow your curves but that are not too clingy. Avoid large patterns at all times.

Proportions

Proportions are quite often ignored when it comes to style. However, getting this right is almost as important as knowing your style. Proportion is the relationship between your torso and your legs, as well as the position of your waist. Once you understand your body proportions you will be able to use colour contrast that will balance out the two parts of the body to create visual balance.

To find out if you are high- or low-waisted, place your hands on your natural waistline and stand in front of a mirror. Then, place your flat hand underneath your bust and the other below it, if you can easily place two hands width ways between your bust and waistline, you are low-waisted and may be slightly shorter on the leg. If you struggle to place the second hand, you are high-waisted and have long legs. If you can fit approximately one and a half hands in, your proportions are

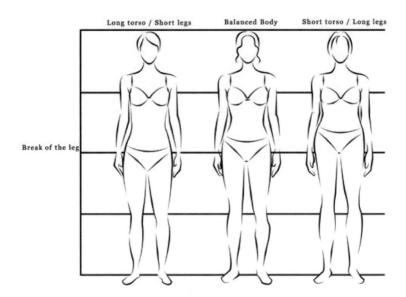

Once you find out if you have short, long or balanced body proportions, you can decide where to 'place' your waistline.

perfectly balanced. You may feel that you have a large bottom, but it could be that you are long in the rise, that is the distance from leg break to the waist.

The recommendations for creating a perfectly proportioned body are fairly simple; if you have a short torso and long legs, avoid tucking in tops and wear low rise pants as well as skirts with no waistbands. And if you have long torso and short legs, do tuck in tops and wear high rise skirts and pants. The key is to deviate the attention from your 'real' waistline.

Chapter 3

Fabrics

Fabrics play a huge role in creating an impeccable image. A well-chosen fabric can determine how the flow of the garments will create structure where it is required, or the right fabric can simply follow the body's natural curves without adding any unnecessary volume. Overall, the type of fabric you choose will largely determine how your outfit will ultimately look. Choosing the right fabrics according to your particular frame is extremely important in creating an appropriate result. For example, thick, heavy, bulky fabrics on a small frame can be overwhelming because of the disparity between the person's relatively smaller size and weight.

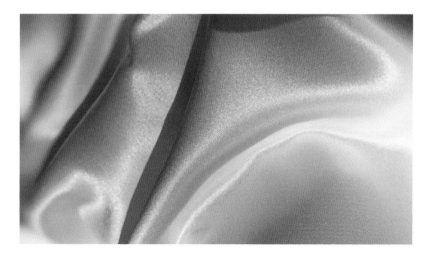

Layering is another great styling tool that, once dominated, can work really well to camouflage some flaws and enhance one's assets (which is the essential principle being communicated here). Not only does layering smooth out the figure, but it can also draw the attention away from 'problem' areas and direct the eye to areas we would prefer to draw attention to. Again, clothing is an important medium through which we can influence how we are perceived by others.

Through fabrics we have the opportunity to make our personality shine. Fabrics not only provide textures to a garment; they can also determine whether we look assertive or approachable. Stiff, firm fabrics in combination with other elements of style can send the message of assertiveness and austerity while more pliable, soft fabrics that follow the body's natural curves result in a more harmonious and approachable look. Thus, fabrics are crucial in the creation of a desirable image.

Judith Rasband, in her book *Wardrobe Strategies for Women*, devoted an entire chapter to fabric selection and coordination. For now, I will simply highlight some essential elements that she presented in order to provide some basic information and principles to consider when choosing the fabrics most suited to you. I would encourage anyone with a keen interest in wanting to review and renew their wardrobes to seek out her book.

Combining Fabrics

The combination of different fabric can add interest to an otherwise uninspiring outfit, and the combination of two similar kinds of fabrics can create a more conservative, formal look. Velvet, satin and sequins are associated with festive, dressy and glamorous occasions, but the difference in their surface textures adds interest to the whole outfit. The same is true in the combination of denim, linen and leather. These natural fabrics (or material, in the case of leather) and textures can work in a way to provide reinforcement to a casual outfit.

The general rule of thumb for fabrics is to create a harmonious and interesting look, and to combine fabrics of different textures. When choosing the fabric that is most suited to you, consider the following:

- Combine a mix of varied textured fabrics along with opaque, solid fabrics
- Ensure quality weaves or knits
- Choose fabrics that keep their shape
- Pick fabrics that retain their original texture
- Select fabrics that flow over the figure without clinging.

Avoid at all costs:

- Monochromatic mixes of flat fabrics or conflicting mixes of textured fabrics
- Mesh, fishnet or see-through fabrics on all but 'costume' occasions
- Poor quality wool or knit that easily pills
- Saggy, baggy or fabrics that lose their shape
- Clingy fabrics

When choosing a certain fabric, you should have in mind your body type, the occasion, or time of the day. Otherwise, you may feel uncomfortable in your outfit, and it will show. The fabric may be too shiny, clingy, see-through, or wrinkly, and you will be self-conscious and uncomfortable. For example: you may be wearing lightweight jersey that is pliable and unforgiving. This might mark your underwear and you will end up pulling the skirt down constantly. The fabrics may be too bulky and overwhelming for your petite frame. A stiff fabric may impede you from moving comfortably when you are presenting a project. So, it's best to experiment with fabrics to discover which ones are most in line with your personal preferences, lifestyle and goals.

Patterns

Patterns are one of the most fun tools to play with and can make a simple outfit more interesting. Patterns are also a great way to show your personality. Like accessories and fabric weight, where we have to take into account the size of the figure, here you should know that the smaller the figure, the smaller and daintier the pattern should be. Remember that patterns can make things appear larger. This has to do with the intensity of the contrast in the pattern, as well as the size of the pattern

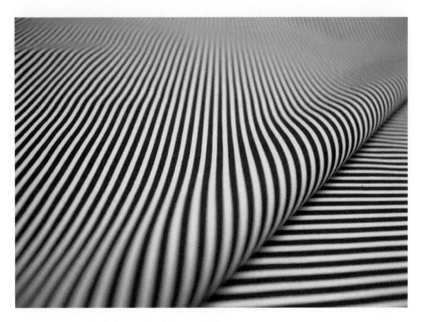

Stripes are one of the most classic patterns.

itself. For a slimming effect, choose a dark background. If you want something to appear larger, the opposite holds true. Patterns can be interesting but also can age you and overwhelm your figure, something we want to avoid.

If you opt for wearing patterns, the best choices are the classic, timeless ones like polka dots, checks, stripes and florals. These patterns are flexible, never fall out of style, and they reflect sophistication. However, patterns should be limited to a few pieces and not make up the bulk of your wardrobe. A wardrobe should predominantly consist of neutral, solid-coloured pieces. A major function of pattern is to break the monotony of a solid outfit. They also help you look current, but they also can make you appear too informal, so it is important to keep an eye on what's available at any given time.

In addition, patterns are also great at creating illusions. The whole point of the elements of style is to create an illusion of a perfect, balanced figure. An illusion is a way of 'fooling' the eyes, creating a false perception or interpretation of something we see. Patterns help us create a sought-after illusion. For example, when we see from a distance someone wearing a vertically striped top, the person appears to be slimmer. Whenever we wear patterns, we are drawing attention to that area and thus emphasising it, which is good for taking attention away from 'problem' areas, as already mentioned. However, it is important to know which areas we want to draw attention to as some areas such as bust, waist, stomach, hips or buttocks generally draw negative attention. This is particularly inappropriate for office and authority roles.

When it comes to mixing patterns, there is an old rule: 'never mix patterns.' I say, forget this! Rules are made to be broken. Once you have acquired a certain knowledge of yourself and what works for you, you will be able to mix patterns that translate into the same motif, mood or theme, and will be completely fine together. They can belong to the same colour family but have different sizes or be same pattern and size but a different colour family. But of course, mixing

Avoid patterns that are too trendy or have motifs, they can make you appear too informal.

*Polka dots along with stripes and paisleys is
also a very classic pattern.*

patterns can look a bit overdone depending on how formal your industry is, so good sense applies at all times.

In summary, one of two elements – motif, colour or size – can be different as long as you highlight only one element. For example, try a small polka dot scarf on a plain top paired with a checked jacket. If you feel comfortable with that, go ahead and try a patterned suit with a patterned shirt, like a medium check suit and a small striped shirt. If you want to play it safe, you can try designer's mixes. These are your ready-to-go patterns to start experimenting with.

Chapter 4

Colour Changes Everything

I wanted to dedicate an entire chapter to the subject of colour because it is one of the most amazing tools that we should master to influence our state of mind and, most importantly, create a long-lasting impression. For me, it doesn't just have an aesthetic connotation.

Colour has intrigued me since I was very young. As I said before, I was once obsessed with colours and that lasted for many years, which made me wonder why that was. So, I went on a mission to find out all about colour, and guess what? I discovered a whole world of information that I am happy to share with you. One of the first things I came across was an article on the psychologist Carl Jung, whom I greatly respect. The article said that he encouraged his patients to use colour to help them express some of the deepest parts of their psyche. It is believed that the colours you choose reflect your personality traits. The colours you pick on a given day also demonstrate your particular mood on that day.

Colour and Style

Leatrice Eiserman and E.P. Cutler suggest in their book *Pantone on Fashion* that, more than any other factor, colour can give a piece of clothing both a visual and emotional impact. Colour communicates everything from mood and personality and there is ample evidence of the psychological impact of colour on our arousal levels which informs how we feel in the presence of certain colours.

If you notice the advertising on any media, you will see that they mostly use colour to send a message. Whatever message they want to transmit, they will always do so with due consideration to the choice of colour. If it is a message of love, they usually use soft hues such as pink, and if it is aimed to alert or alarm, they often use warm bright hues such as red or yellow. Colours have tremendous historical significance, and many colours have been associated with clear and profound meanings throughout the years. Red has often been associated with intense emotion, whereas white conjures up a feeling of purity.

We often choose colour unconsciously, based on our personal taste, and consistent with the other aspects of our style. Once you get familiar with your personal elements of style, choosing what is right for you becomes a whole lot easier, and you can eventually enjoy experimenting with variations that can reflect emerging trends while remaining consistent with what works best for you. I will share more details on personal style later on. With colour, there are three aspects to consider. First, we need to consider the aesthetic aspects. Second, you must determine which correspond to you most. Finally, the psychological aspects require appreciation, as it very often determines what impact you want to make, both on others and on how you wish to feel about yourself.

Some make-up concepts teach that there are warm, cool and neutral skin tones that you should be aware of when choosing foundation and overall products. Reason being that colour can make us look younger, more rested, and slimmer. There are practically no limits to what colour can do to our overall look.

Aesthetically speaking, the same concept applies for clothing. There is no need to know every single colour that suits you personally. All you need to know is whether you have a warm, cool or neutral undertone. There are a few easy ways to find out your skin's undertone. One common way is by checking the colour of your veins on the back of your wrist. If they appear blue, your undertone is cool, and if it is olive, it is warm. If you struggle to conclude which colour you are, that means you probably have a neutral undertone. Another strategy is to bring a piece of white paper next to your face and compare it with your colouring; if you have a cool undertone, you may appear bluer than the paper and if you have a yellow undertone, you may appear yellower than the paper. If you are warm (yellow), the colours you wear should have a yellow base to them (e.g., olive greens, orange-reds, earthy tones such as browns and coppers). On the other hand, if you have a cool undertone, your colours should have a blue base to them such as purple-red, turquoise and violet, for instance.

You also have to consider contrast, namely the contrast between your complexion, hair and eye colour, this is very important as it will determine the intensity of the hues to be used. A low contrast is determined by fair hair and skin and pale, light eyes. A deep contrast is determined by fair skin and dark hair or eyes.

As a stylist, I have considered the effects of colours on different complexions and body shapes and how they can enhance or cast harsh shadows, not suiting one complexion or making a particular part of the body appear smaller than it really is. But I don't think it is of vital importance to build an entire wardrobe based on the colours that suit you today. There are a number of factors that limit this analysis, such as hair colour dyeing or how one gets paler or tanned throughout the year, etc. There will be days when you will want to wear a determined colour, that in theory doesn't suit you, and feel a certain way.

Dispelling Myths

It has been suggested that the meanings and associations with colour have conditioned us for a long time. Take red, for instance. The colour red has long been associated with power, strength and confidence. Unfortunately, there is little evidence to the effects of colour on our mood and perception of self and others.

We may still have strong attachments to stereotypes and, at times, may want to pay attention to these. Due to the lack of scientific evidence, we can also remain open and flexible with regards to colour and the psychological effect on others' views of us. What is more important is that our colour choices complement our tone and body types, instead of feeling restricted by preconceived views of the messages various colours may convey.

Once you know what image you wish to portray, and have chosen the desired colour(s), you need to combine the right colours to create a harmonious look. Colours from the same family or monochromatic colour schemes only vary in terms of values and hue (i.e., when you add white or black to them). Adjacent colours are the ones that sit next to each other on the colour wheel (see next section), and complementary colours are the ones that sit opposite to each other. So how do we choose colours that really work well together?

The Colour Wheel

The Colour Wheel organises colours around a circle to demonstrate the relationship between primary, secondary and tertiary colours. To create harmonious colour combinations, you can consider using any two, three or even four colours opposite to each other on the colour wheel (essentially forming a rectangle i.e., two pairs of colours opposite one another). These harmonious colour combinations are called colour schemes – sometimes the term 'colour harmonies' is also used.

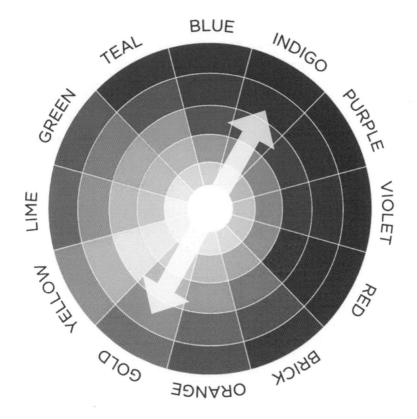

For example, when you choose an indigo blue skirt and a camel sweater, or a salmon top paired with an aqua green pair of pants, you are matching colours opposite to one another on the colour wheel. You will notice that I am favouring colours with the same depth, but it doesn't need to be this way. You can also choose opposite colours with different depth (for example, bright yellow and lilac). All you have to do is follow the arrow with the corresponding colour palette that is across from the other end, and then you can play with the depth of the hues as well, going from the lighter to the darker ones.

Every year Pantone elects a colour for the year which is then taken up by the fashion industry. The Pantone Colour Institute is a consulting service within Pantone© that forecasts global colour trends and advises companies on colour and brand identity and product development. The Pantone Colour Institute partners with global brands to leverage the power, psychology and emotion of colour in their design strategy.

This becomes much more than 'setting trends' as we are becoming more fascinated with colour and recognise its ability to convey deep messages and meanings. As such, designers and brands are now feeling empowered to use colour to inspire and influence in a multitude of ways.

Using Colour

Monochromatic

Combining monochromatic looks create a subtle and sophisticated look. Using colours of the same family or adjacent can create a soft transition from one another and add interest to the look or to complementary colours for maximum impact. Darker monochromatic outfits have a slimming effect on the result, while light ones result in the contrary effect. High contrast monochromatic schemes, for instance, black and white, can have an exciting effect besides having a functional aspect of creating balance in the overall look.

A black monochromatic outfit can lend a slimming effect.

A light monochromatic outfit although very chic can make you appear larger.

*A neutral monochromatic look
is sophisticated and offers a soft
transition.*

*Colour contrast is the use of
dark/light to create balance in
the overall look.*

Colour contrast

Another very useful tool is to consider colour contrast, where one colour will prevail upon another by weakening its effect. For instance, when you wear something red and pair it with beige, red appears to be less vibrant. That way you draw the attention to yourself, say for a presentation or meeting, without being too assertive.

However, when you pair a vibrant colour with black or white, it appears brighter, as shown in the picture

You may have heard of colour blocking. It's a term that all fashionistas love to use. Colour blocking is the use of colours that are opposite to each other to create a harmonious result. For instance, if you wear a red skirt and a green top, you are colour blocking. Doesn't that remind you of a Christmas tree? Those colours were put together to incite harmony. These colours can be very stimulating, but by dulling or varying the intensity of the hues a more calming effect is achieved.

Another way of using colour contrast is referring to the make-up concept of contour and highlight. We use bright light colours to bring an element forward to highlight it and make it more evident, and dark solid colours to make it appear smaller and recede. When we use colours that are opposite in value, i.e., bright/dark, we can create visual balance by creating a

Red appears less vibrant when paired with soft neutral colours, such as beige.

Red appears more vibrant when paired with black or white.

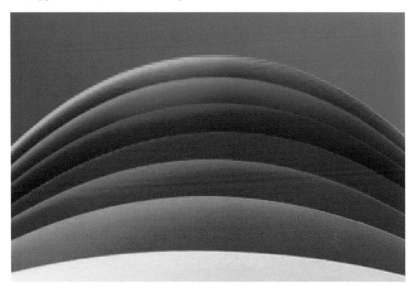

Colour blocking is the exploration of the opposite colours of the colour wheel placed together.

Example of a soft colour blocking.

An example of colour blocking.

Not everyone can wear total black well.

desirable illusion. For instance, we can minimise large hips and narrow shoulders by the use of a dark solid colour on the bottom half and bright light colours on the top half.

When we want to draw attention to a certain part of our body, we can wear bright, light colours, such as a yellow satin piece for instance. If we want to make something appear smaller, we should wear dark, solid colours instead. The rule of thumb is dark solid colours disguise volume, while light bright colours make it appear larger.

Black for everyone

Despite the subtitle, black is not for everyone. Black can be pretty harsh with certain complexions as well as against more mature skin. Also, the texture, type of fabrics, and how much skin you show will soften or harden black's effect. Knits and satins will lighten a black outfit. To appear slimmer, you should wear your best colours, only darker, in a monochromatic outfit. It is better to be inclusive rather than exclusive. If you love black, there are a few ways to make it work for you. So, take of note the following rules:

Wear a light top and dark bottom if you have a pear body type.

1. Remember your undertone? If you are warm, go back to your best colours and wear them close to your face. For instance, if you are wearing a black leather jacket, put on a T-shirt or a scarf underneath that has one of your best colours. If you are cool, use a cool base piece or some silver jewellery.

2. Having the above rule in mind, also take into consideration how soft or deep you are. Look at yourself in the mirror and notice the contrast between your skin, hair and eyes. Do they transition smoothly, or is there a contrast between them? For example, are they all light, or do you have dark hair with pale skin and light eyes? If you have a soft contrast, choose light hues. If you have deep contrast, you should wear light and dark colours together, such as a black and white striped shirt.

3. Unless you have depth to your overall look, such as dark eyes, skin and hair, you can't wear black around your face successfully. Following the above tips, as well as showing a bit of skin in the right places, such as an open neckline for example, will soften the effect of black.

Wear a dark top and light bottom if you have an inverted triangle body type.

How do you want to be perceived?

Once we know what colours and styles suit us best, it is time to start thinking of how we want people to perceive us, as well as how we want to feel. Let your closet work for your professional image with the right dose of classic and trendy pieces.

When we are meeting a client at a conference or attending any other social or professional events, it is crucial to look into the dress code, the culture of the organisation, and the personal style of who you will be interacting with. It is a mistake to impose our personal style on others. Of course, we can and should express our individuality, but when it comes to adhering to a professional agenda, adjusting our own style to others is a more appropriate way to behave. You have to resonate with that individual, and there is no better way to achieve that than having an immediate impact on how they perceive us through our clothes. A combination of all the elements of style, including colour, can create a powerful end result in achieving that goal. In these instances, bright hues will definitely create an impactful memory if that is your goal. Soft hues will result in a more approachable you.

Wearing a vibrant colour with black makes it appear more vibrant and will draw the attention to it.

47

A neutral outfit with soft lines can make you appear more approachable.

Red can make you appear more assertive.

Chapter 5

Price per wear: Divide the price of the item by the number of times you wear it per week.

Quality

The core of our wardrobe should consist of the best quality pieces that have perennial classic styles to them. Thus, it becomes of paramount importance to focus on choosing quality pieces as part of your wardrobe. Please remember that quality

does not necessarily come with a steep price tag. There are affordable brands that have very good quality items through the use of good fabric and attention to detail. When it comes to dressing impeccably, quality is the number one aspect of a garment. We should therefore be able to recognise quality by looking at an item on the rack. But first things first: what is quality?

What is quality?

Quality can mean different things to different people. A quality garment should be durable and last for many seasons. Quality must consider tailoring, the fabric, and seams. Although these aspects can be quite technical, there's no need to feel overwhelmed. You can always come back to this book for reference when needed.

As mentioned before, a quality garment should last for many seasons without losing its shape or colour, regardless of how many times you wear it, wash it or dry-clean it. It should fit your body shape and not distort or restrict you in any way. Most importantly, it should feel comfortable, as we don't want fabrics that peel, fade, rip, or have buttons pop out. For this to be possible, all the components must work together: fabric, seams, lining, tailoring, and all other details.

The quality of a garment is only as good as the care and attention put into the making. High quality garments usually take a long time to make and as such can cost much more. Cheap pieces look great on the rack and are meant to look great on the rack *only*. Most consumers only take this into consideration after they have already purchased the piece. They look at the item on the rack without analysing it in depth, checking seams, how it's been tailored, its fabric, etc.

My number one tip is that, whenever possible, it is essential to see the piece in the flesh. It's much easier to feel its quality when you touch it as opposed to just seeing images of it. This is the main disadvantage of buying garments online, as you are looking at an image rather than seeing the real thing. It is important that you try it on to see if the fit is right for you and how it feels to the touch. Yet, with that said, I have added some of the best online shops at the end of this book for guidance and for your convenience. I have used most of them myself. They have a 24/7 customer service, provide the items' measurements, mention if the item is generous in size and show a close-up photo of the garment. Remember, a good online purchase is only possible if you know your body very well and know fabric names, and even then, there are no guarantees.

Recognising quality and investing in quality pieces doesn't mean that your entire wardrobe should consist only of high-quality pieces. Let's be realistic! You need a clear strategy around which quality items you will invest in and incorporate into your wardrobe.

Let's start with fabrics. The fabric of a garment is the most important component of its quality. You should look out for the quality of the fabric itself and then how suitable it is for that particular item. Compare two pieces of the same fabric, say cotton, and notice the difference. In some cases, the difference can be huge.

Cotton

Good quality cotton should be soft, pliable and durable. The most important property of good cotton is its length. Long cotton fibres are considered a better quality because it is tightly bound, making it stronger and more durable. These are also softer, because longer fibres are easier to spin into yarn.

Breathability is also a beneficial feature of cotton. Good quality cotton breathes more because it contains air pockets between the individual threads. And, as a natural fabric, cotton is also easier to maintain as it is washable. Some of the best-known long thread cottons are Prima, Sea-Island and Egyptian.

You can recognise a good quality cotton if it is:

- well built
- does not pill, and
- is less transparent.

The great news is that you can find affordable cotton garments because they are relatively cheap to produce.

Linen

Linen is made from flax fibres that are naturally smooth and at the same time not very elastic. Linen is great for hot days, as it is breathable and good for cooling. Because of this it also dries quickly.

You can feel a good quality linen if it:

- feels pleasant on the skin, and
- it wrinkles very easily (but it should look ok at the end of the day).

Wool

The quality of wool is determined by the diameter and the quality of the individual wool fibres that make up the fabric. The breed of the animal that produced the wool also plays a huge role in its quality. Finer wool grades are typically more expensive than coarser wool fibres as they are softer and more difficult to manufacture. You can also recognise a good quality wool when there aren't any knots present.

One has to bear in mind that almost all wool pills, but because high quality wool variants are more tightly woven, this prevents fibres from becoming loose. So, check to see if there are any pills on a garment when you are trying it on, and if not, that's a good indication of the quality (at least in the first instance). You also should not be able to see through the garment. Finally, some types of wool are naturally softer than others (e.g., cashmere is softer than mohair), so the softness of a wool item does not always speak for its quality.

Denim

The quality of denim depends on the quality of the cotton used to manufacture it. You should be able to recognise a good quality denim if it:
- feels soft and almost like it's a little moist
- isn't too thin or stiff, but conforms to your body's natural curves

- isn't so thin that it will tear easily or too stiff that it will prevent movement, and
- has seams that do not split or unravel under stress because denim is very heavy fabric.

And remember, the one thing that drives prices up in the denim manufacturing is its wash. This doesn't translate into quality but can impact the longevity of the product if it is heavily treated.

Leather

Although leather is a material rather than a fabric, I think it is important to highlight its qualities as well. The quality of a leather piece depends on the kind of 'grain' it has. Full grain is considered the highest quality and refers to untreated leather that maintains the skin's natural fibre strength and durability. The other two types (top-grain and split grain) are processed, making them less durable and lacking that patina quality over time. You should recognise a good quality leather piece if its grains look natural or printed. High quality natural leather has all the natural imperfections from the animal's skin (Rees, 2014).

Synthetics

There are a few advantages to synthetic materials. One advantage is the low cost of manufacturing. Another one is the similarity to natural fibres. Some designers will choose synthetic materials due to their weight and functionality. When blended with natural fibres, synthetics can actually improve the fit of an otherwise natural fabric. Spandex, polyester and Lycra all add elasticity to naturally stiff fabrics like cotton and wool. There are types of garments that are best made of synthetic fibres, such as active wear, due to their elasticity.

Regardless of the type of fabric, it is important to note that:
- the shoulder line should fall right at the curve of the shoulders
- pleats, pockets and lapels should all lie flat and not protrude, and
- the inside lining and structure should be stiff enough to hold the shape of the garment.

Getting the Fit Right

The second aspect of quality I would like to explore is the particular fit of your items to achieve the most flattering result.

As an overall rule, we should aim for our clothes to fit our bodies closely and choose the more classic styles. Unless, of course, it's purposely tailored for a looser cut, such as puffy sleeves, for instance. When trying on an item you have to take into account the length and the amount of vertical or drag lines across the garment. As I shared earlier, the garment should finish at the narrowest part of the body and it shouldn't have vertical lines, which imply that there is too much fabric.

Bear in mind that the fashion industry is trying to cater to a diverse population with a huge variety of body types so the fitting of a garment can be very generic and not suit the important physical characteristics of a person's actual body.

When it comes to our wardrobes, we must pay particular attention to the fit and suitability of our mainstay items that we will likely choose to wear the most and among the most important is our jeans.

Jeans

The quality of your jeans is closely linked to its fit as well as the cotton it's made of. As well, there are so many styles to choose from that can be overwhelming to find the right one for your frame. Be open minded and patient, and you will most definitely find the perfect one for you.

The first thing to observe when trying on a pair is if they go on too easily, if they do then go down a size as jeans will always stretch. Try to sit down or even squat for a while and feel how comfortable they are.

A bit of stretch (cotton/polyester blend) is recommended specially if you have curvy hips or thighs. Normally stretch jeans have between 1% to 3% elastane, but some brands go up to 4%. The amount of stretch is completely personal and the stretchier the jeans are then the more form-fitting the jeans should be when you purchase them. Remember that with additional stretch, the jeans will lose their shape more quickly in-between washes.

Don't worry about 'whiskering', the thin fading lines formed from creases that are usually found on the front pocket area of jeans. They add interest and depth on

Jeans whiskering.

Same goes with size! Some brands are more generous than others. So, try not to pay attention to "the number" and focus on the actual fit as this is the most important aspect. Keep in mind that if you can fit two fingers down the back of the waist then it is likely a sign that you have a good fit to start with.

When having your jeans hemmed make sure the tailor always measures them from your heel, otherwise they may come back too short. The hem should fall in the middle of the heel. These two rules apply for any pants, by the way. And ensure the tailor is able to finish the hem the way the jeans had been finished to begin with. The little details are important. When having any pants hemmed take the shoes you want to wear with them to the fitting and that includes your jeans. You should decide on the shoes and stick with those shoes. Stick with shoes that are similar in height so that the jeans will fit properly given the length that they were hemmed. Remember that cropped jeans can also be hemmed. If they are too long (go past your mid-calf) they will make you appear shorter.

When choosing your jeans, the following are a few final points to consider ensuring they will compliment your body the best:

- Look for a curved waistband that will be slightly higher at the back than the front and as this will curve into your waist rather than sit straight up.
- Tall girls look best in a mid-waist jean at the right height, whereas petite girls look great in a high-rise jean that accentuates the waist and elongates the legs.

Pay attention to the placement of the pockets.

- The yoke or riser is the 'V" shape section at the back of the jeans, which gives them their curved seat. This 'V' shape will determine how big the curve is depending on how deep it is. High waisted jeans without a yoke can make the bottom look longer.
- The placement and size of the pockets, particularly in a bootleg style, is also essential. Look for big pockets placed just above the crease of the bottom for a more flattering effect.
- Premium jeans can be expensive, and like any other item, you should take care of them. Only wash in cold water as the quality of detergents will not require anything more. Hot water and jeans are not friends.
- Pear shaped or curvy ladies who like skinny jeans should look at high waisted styles - it elongates the leg and slims down the hip.

Blazer

The blazer is another very popular and versatile item that requires special attention to how it's been made. This includes the fabric, the interior details, the lapels, pockets and cuff.

When trying on a blazer, notice if the shoulder line finishes right at the curve of the shoulder. Cross your arms and feel how snug it is. You shouldn't feel restrained.

A blazer can be dressed down with jeans.

Check the lining and what fabric is used, satin is the most common. Check also if there's any structure to the blazer as this will determine the longevity of the item.

Premium blazers can be expensive, and with all of your investment items, you should take care really good care of them. Check the tags before washing them but most blazers will require professional dry cleaning only.

In terms of size, a well-fitting blazer should be relatively loose around the bust and the length should be one that doesn't fall in the widest part of the body, and the lapel and pockets should lie flat.

The length of the sleeves on women's blazer is a bit more flexible than for men. Women can have a three-quarter length or full length or even a short sleeve blazer. However, if opting for full length, make sure it just touches the thumb.

Pear shaped or curvy ladies look best in styles that have shoulder pads to structure them and make them squarer and balanced.

Shirt

The fit of a shirt follows some of the blazer principles in that the line should fall right at the curve of the shoulders. The size

is very important as you don't want to have your movements constricted, but there should not be a gap between your buttons at any time. The collar must fall flat and keep their shape after many washes, so pay extra attention to the interlining of the shirt to make sure it's crisp and firm.

Dressed for an important business transaction.

Sequin dresses for after-hours cocktails.

Dressed for a job interview.

Chapter 6

Dressing for the occasion

Most people tend to dress either according to their mood on a given day, their typical style, or based on their age. We tend to dress in our usual clothes and style them our usual way. When we dress for the office, we forget a very important rule: dress for whom you are interacting with. Of course, the industry you work in will naturally determine how much you can express your individuality. But it is important to always remember that you need to portray the most professional image possible to everyone that you come into contact with. Whether you have a job interview, are visiting a client, sales prospect, your business partner, or a colleague in your workspace, you should express your personal preferences while conforming to the situation and/or circumstances you are in. In this way you will always create harmony and not discrepancy in your professional environment.

If you are underdressed, you run the risk of looking unprofessional, or too laid back and disinterested. If you are overdressed, you can make others uncomfortable. Before your interview or meeting, do a search on the company profile and the person you are meeting with. Thanks to social media, it is easy to gather this information easily. Find out their style: classic, modern, conservative, etc. Review the company's values, mission and vision to assist with the process of discovering how you should present yourself for an important meeting or interview. That does not mean you cannot be yourself. You can always add a personal touch. This is very important and can be in the form of an accessory like a scarf with a beautiful and sophisticated print or a pattern, or a piece of jewellery. Dressing for the occasion means you are dressed professionally. People will respect you more and value your input. If you have a cocktail party after hours, you can always change when you finish your workday.

When we dress for our body, our age, the environment we are in, and who we are interacting with, we aren't distracted and can focus on what we're really good at. Our confidence level shows and people are drawn to us and can relate to us, because we are giving them our full attention.

Have you ever felt that you were under/overdressed for an occasion? You hardly felt like interacting with anyone because you were self-conscious. You can rest assured that people felt the same towards you. Not only because you dressed inappropriately, but also because you felt bad about yourself, which showed. It becomes a vicious cycle.

In these moments you have lost an opportunity to create a long-lasting impression, and we often do not get a second chance. Appearance is very important. A 2010 national poll, conducted by the Centre for Professional Excellence at York College of Pennsylvania, asked respondents to name qualities most often associated with professionalism. Appearance ranked second, after communication skills. Matthew Randall, Executive Director of the CPE, suggested that "how an individual dresses for work can be a powerful extension of his personal brand. Clothes, accessories and even the footwear an employee chooses to wear helps to reinforce or diminish his skills and qualities in the eyes of his employer, co-workers and clients."

HOT TIP

THE SIZE OF THE
ACCESSORIES SHOULD
BE ACCORDING TO
THE PERSON'S FRAME
THEREFORE, THE
SMALLER THE FRAME
THE SMALLER THE
ACCESSORIES.

Chapter 7

The Final Touches

Accessories can completely change an outfit. They are the final touches, and they also give you many possibilities to  showcase your uniqueness, your signature look! Another very important aspect of accessories is that they draw attention away from our less-than-perfect areas. They can make us look current, youthful, chic, and much more. And because they are single pieces, they are a smart way to elevate our wardrobe while saving us money, as they cost less than an entire outfit. Inappropriate accessories can make you look outdated, add unnecessary bulk, and even emphasise our little flaws. Everything we don't want!

When we wear a bold accessory as the focal point of an outfit, we should let the rest of the outfit be more neutral to not compete with it. So, here are some tips on how to choose the right accessories for our particular self or occasion:

Shoes:

When it comes to shoes, special attention is required. Having good quality shoes is of critical importance to ensure you are looking after your health. Opt for shoes that are made by shoemakers. Try to avoid overly 'fashionable' shoes, as they tend

HOT TIP

A BEAUTIFULLY STYLED
SCARF, A SPECIAL BELT,
THE RIGHT ACCESSORY CAN
TRANSFORM AN OTHERWISE
MUNDANE OUTFIT INTO
SOMETHING EXTRAORDINARY.
ON THE OTHER HAND, IT
CAN ALSO RUIN THE
WHOLE LOOK.

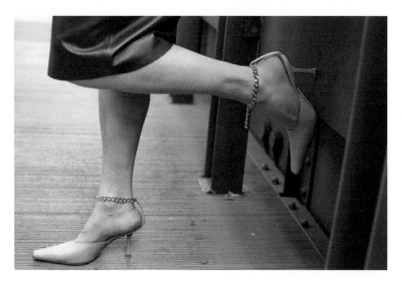

to be designed to just look good and do not respect the feet's anatomy. There is nothing more unattractive than someone who cannot walk in high heels.

In the office: classics like pumps and sling backs are always a great choice. If your company is more liberal, you can adventure into platforms or even sneakers, in the case of marketing/creative areas. Pointed toes elongate the legs and always look more polished.

After hours/weekends: The sky is the limit but, as a rule, regardless of where you will wear your shoes, they should still be quality shoes to walk in.

Shoes should always be comfortable. Make sure you try both shoes in a pair on and walk around the shop before you buy. If you have wide feet, look for the right width for your feet as well.

HOT TIP

POINTED TOES SHOES
ARE MORE FLATTERING
AND ELONGATING THAN
ROUND ONES.

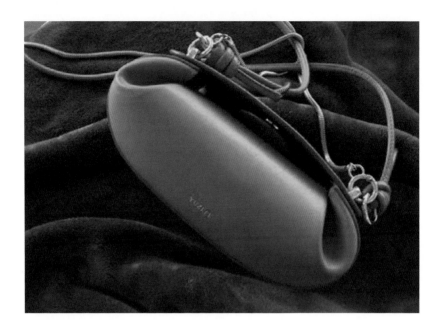

Handbags:

The possibilities surrounding handbags are limitless. There are many classic and extremely expensive bags out there, but there is no need to have an entire collection of designer handbags. Younger girls can get away with having a bit of fun and more relaxed handbags. As we scale up the ladder in the corporate world, we need to pay more attention to our accessories, and handbags are no exception. Investing in a classic structured genuine leather handbag is crucial. That doesn't mean it has to be boring and you can show a bit of personality. Having one or two really well made in solid neutral colours is an important starting point. If you want to have fun and play with the season's trends, do it on the weekends!

Sunglasses: Like shoes, having the right sunglasses is good for your health. You have to have the highest quality possible so that they provide UVA and UVB protection. When looking for the right shape for you, try to counterbalance your face shape. For example, if you have a round or oblong face, try something rectangular. If you have a square face, try round frames. The smaller your face the smaller the glasses should be, and vice versa.

Belts: Way beyond the function to hold pants and skirts, belts are crucial when the goal is creating shape. By adding a belt, you highlight a waist that would otherwise disappear, making you appear larger than you actually are. Belts also draw attention to them, so it becomes easy to disguise areas that we want to de-emphasise. As a rule, a small frame person should wear thin belts, whereas a taller person can get away with thicker belts.

Scarves: Scarves bring pops of colour and texture to an outfit. You should invest in pliable fabrics, because they fall much better and are soft on the skin compared to stiffer ones. The size and colour of the prints are very important because they frame and reflect light right back to your face. So always try a few on and see how they feel and look. But don't limit the use of scarves to the neck! They can be worn around handbags, wrists or as headbands if you want to be more creative.

Use a belt to highlight a waist and add interest at the same time.

New ways of wearing a scarf as shown here.

Jewellery: The older we get, the less costume-like our jewellery should be. Opt for dainty pieces that resemble real jewellery as much as possible. Whenever you can, wear real jewellery, including watches, earrings, bracelets, and rings with semi-precious stones and gems. These should be investment buys that show refinement and attention to detail, which is important from a career perspective.

HOT TIP

CHOOSE GOLDEN
JEWELLERY IF YOU HAVE A
WARM SKIN UNDERTONE
AND SILVER IF YOU HAVE
A COOL UNDERTONE.

Style vs. Trend

For me it is of critical importance that we are able to differentiate between what is a style and what is a trend. If you are one of those people who say: "I don't have style," think again. Whether you are aware of it or not, style comes naturally. Have a look around and see your furniture, for instance. Is it classic or modern? What's your ideal holiday look like? Is it a resort at a quiet beach, or shopping in a busy city? As girls, many of us dream of our wedding dress. Will it be princess like? Or mermaid shape? Style is every single choice you make. It is not only how we dress, but it also encompasses all aspects of our lives, as mentioned by Gloria Khalil in her book *Chic*. Our culture, our values, and our view of the world also shape our style. It is what makes us who we are. It is our uniqueness. Many people are not aware of it. Style stays with us, yet also evolves throughout our lives, as our body changes and we get to know ourselves better.

When we know our own unique style, we can use the ideas and suggestions introduced by the industry without just *swallowing them*. Once you know what your style is and what works for you, you will be able to mitigate the influence of the fashion industry. To know you style, you simply have to ask yourself: Who do I look up to? Who do I find stylish? A celebrity, a friend... is she always wearing trends or classic pieces? Is she Romantic? Modern? Edgy? Eclectic?

Notice the pieces that are predominant in your wardrobe. How do you describe them? Once you find out what your style is, you will make clearer decisions. Stylish people have developed a great deal of self-esteem because they are not dictated by external factors. But it is important to know that for our personal style to work well for us, we need to know what we are doing. Our choices need to be informed, structured and organised and, above all, we have to attend to all the changes that occur within us and around us. Otherwise, it's just *a* choice rather than the *right* choice.

Having an amazing personal style isn't about wearing logos. After all, we are not billboards, right? So, when trends emerge, we are capable of knowing how we put them together while incorporating them into who we already are. And as I mentioned before, regardless of your bank account, if you have a true sense of style, you will always be fashionable.

"Being well dressed doesn't have much to do with having good clothes. It's a question of good balance and common sense."
Oscar De La Renta

Trend, on the other hand, results from suggestions that stem from the fashion industry. And there are many trends out there at any one time. A trend can be considered the commercial part of fashion and is thus transient and often elusive. Every season, creative directors from the most influential fashion houses select the colours, fabrics and design elements for their brand. This is done to create a sense of urgency and instil a need for new things, to keep the wheels of the fashion industry turning. This plays on society-wide needs for conformity and acceptance. It can be said that, at times, we don't know how to dress ourselves for the same reason we don't eat well. The fashion and food industry want to sell their products and we can be easily convinced, unless we have the foundational knowledge to form a critical view on what is being promoted, and then determine its true efficacy and suitability for us.

In fashion the process is quite simple. There is a muse (someone popular who will inspire and influence) who becomes the *trend-setter.* Muses used to be Hollywood stars, then later celebrities, and now they are often bloggers or 'influencers.' They are the original. The followers of trends are the copies.

So, it is important to know how trends work to make conscious, well-informed decisions. From a fashion insider's point of view, if you see a trend worn by micro influencers, you know it's officially over!

And how does a trend hit its peak? First, a trend-setter or mega influencer (someone with over 500k followers) wears it and creates the initial fuss. Mass brands catch on to the trend, create a version of it, and start selling it in retail chains and malls, bringing it down to High Street stores for more affordable and easy access. At this point, it has hit its peak. If you are still unsure if something is on trend, have a look at social media and see who is still wearing it and you will know. So, limit trends to the minimum. They can be a fun part of your wardrobe, making you look current, but do not suit everybody every time.

So, where to save and where to splurge?

The bottom line is that the core of your wardrobe should consist of timeless, quality pieces. There should be no

compromising. They should be investment pieces of the best quality possible. Neutral hues and key pieces that work as the foundation to create different looks should be the stars of your work wardrobe. That doesn't mean they have to be boring and limited to the office though. They can and should navigate to other areas of your life, combined with some more 'trendy' elements. Another way of working your wardrobe is layering pieces in an interesting way and balancing out the masculine/ feminine ratio. The secret for success is allying good taste and sense together.

Investment Buys

Building the foundation

For starters, good quality lingerie is a must. If your underwear is not in good shape, it can easily wreck an entire outfit. The opposite is also true. Good quality underwear that is the right fit can make your outfit appear slimmer and neater. Taking it a step further, you should also invest in shapewear. Nowadays, there are great options that will give the right support, tuck in those little extra bits and make you feel more beautiful, attractive and comfortable. Good lingerie should not mark your skin or be too tight or loose. Ask for help when buying lingerie. Salespeople in department stores are typically well trained. Shapewear as well as underwear are vital for pulling in a round tummy, hip or derriere, which helps create a smoother figure.

Basics such as good quality white cotton t-shirts, shapewear and underwear are must-haves all year round. White t-shirts are the base of many outfits and great for layering. But they must be impeccably white, otherwise they will ruin the look of the whole outfit. Under arm stains or pilled fabric are no nos. When you find quality cotton t-shirts, buy them in bulk. (Please refer to the fabric chapter in order to find out where you can purchase good quality cotton t-shirts).

Below is a list of quality foundation pieces that I recommend you have in your wardrobe:

- White shirt
- Patterned shirt (polka dots, striped or paisley)
- Little black dress
- Skirt
- Tailored trousers
- Dark jeans

White shirt.

Patterned shirt.

Little black dress.

Skirt.

Tailored trousers.   *Wool blazer.*

Coat.

Pumps.

- Black blazer
- Wool blazer
- Coat
- Flats
- Pumps
- Leather handbag

Seasonal wardrobes

The Winter "Must-Haves" checklist:

- Trench coat
- Knits
- Cardigan
- Jackets
- Coats

Trench coat, winter staple.   *Winter coat.*

- Leather pants
- Leather skirt
- Pashmina
- Scarf
- Gloves
- Boots
- Felt hats
- Beanies

The Summer "Must-Haves" checklist:

- Tanks
- Empire tops
- Caftan

- Shorts
- Jumpsuits
- Prints skirts
- Swimsuit
- Summer dresses

Shorts.   *Swimsuit.*

Floral print dress, summer staple.

- Barely-there sandals
- Flat shoes
- Espadrilles
- Hats
- Sunglasses

Barely-there sandals.

Wardrobe Feng Shui

According to this Chinese ancient practice, *the wardrobe shall not be cluttered*! The underlying premise of Feng Shui, according to Tisha Morris (2011), is to harmonise the energy of spaces with the earth's energy. The wardrobe, which is often overlooked, is an important aspect to achieving a healthy balance of flow in the house. Clutter in our wardrobes is a common occurrence that can prevent optimal energy flow and lead to confusion in the mornings when we are getting ourselves ready for our day.

Sure, it's easy to think that because it is out of sight, it is out of mind. But that could not be further from the truth. Just think of how stressed you get when you cannot find anything when you need it the most. Especially when you are running late for that important meeting, the negativity this creates makes for a bad start of your day.

The rules on the organisation of your wardrobe are very easy to follow. Again, Tisha Morris (2011) provides some very practical advice in improving our closets:

- Remove all the clothing to start and only put back the clothes you will actually wear going forward.
- Give it a good clean. Vacuum, dust, and paint, if needed, preferably white.
- Get rid of anything that is not in good condition or that you haven't worn in a while and that does not fit you perfectly.
- Organise – Get some bins, baskets or any type of organiser, so you know exactly where things are, and you won't create clutter when you put things back.
- Align your wardrobe with the seasons and keep the closet in your bedroom clean and organised.
- When you have finished, try to donate one piece for each new article of clothing you buy, to keep everything in balance.

HOT TIP

YOUR WORK WARDROBE
SHOULD BE PERFECTLY FITTING,
COMFORTABLE, MADE OF TECH
FABRICS THAT DON'T WRINKLE.
THIS WAY YOU DON'T NEED
TO WORRY ABOUT HOW YOU
WILL LOOK AT THE END OF
THE DAY.

The Work Wardrobe

As mentioned earlier, the central idea is to help you craft a capsule wardrobe that will look pristine from 9 to 5, and that has passed the wrinkle resistance test! After all, we do move around, or worse, often sit for large periods of time. An ideal wardrobe for work is one that continues to look great throughout the day, and even 'after hours' should we have to meet late with clients or wish to catch up with friends after hours for cocktails.

A winning work wardrobe is full of hero pieces that are timeless, great quality, and personalised. They fit with your position and the organisation's culture yet allow you to express your individuality. When finalising your work wardrobe, consider these essential pieces:

- Separates are your best bets as they allow you to co-ordinate, giving you flexibility, and you will get more wear out of them.

- Stay away from pieces that are too loud. For example, avoid accessories such as bangles or audacious earrings. Same goes for clothing that is very vibrant, too tight, too loose, too short, or too long. And nothing see-through, or with lace or too trendy is recommended. But be careful, as being too conservative can leave the impression of being outdated or lacking personality, which is not ideal for your career advancement. The key is to achieve a balance in attaining a professional image but ensuring that you bring yourself and your style to your work wear.

Except if you are a professional who needs to wear a uniform, you will either belong to a formal or informal group. If you need formal attire for the workplace, consider the following:

- Invest in a good suit. You can add a touch of personality in the form of accessories, but the cut must be impeccable.

- Choose a pant or skirt suit in different colours and fabric weight. Refer to your personal colours to find out which option is best for you.

- Select versatile dresses that you can dress up or down depending on the occasion.

- Buy cardigans, jackets and blazers. They elevate any outfit.

- Make sure shirts and blouses can be worn on their own or underneath jackets and blazers.

- Include good quality knits to wear indoors to be ready for air conditioning.

- Have some quality jewellery that includes a nice wristwatch.

- Buy comfortable shoes but choose ones with great design elements. Remember that with shoes, you will get what you pay for, so make sure they are comfortable and well made.

- Ensure you have a structured, quality leather bag.

Things to Avoid:

- Active wear
- Kaftans, fringed jackets, or any ethnic references
- Cocktail dresses
- Mini dresses or skirts
- Tight or see-through pants that reveal underwear
- Overalls
- Deep décolletage
- Cropped tops
- Flat sandals
- Distressed jeans

Dressing for Interviews

Consistent with the message interwoven throughout the book, first impressions matter. This couldn't be truer when we dress to be interviewed for a role we desire. You will spend a significant amount of time outlining your qualifications and experiences on your resume. To your interviewer this is an opportunity to determine your fit for the organisation and its culture.

An interview is your opportunity to showcase who you are. By dressing your best, you will feel confident and exude poise, clarity and purpose in how you answer the questions. You can thus make the most of the opportunity provided to you. It is essential that you put some thought into the outfit you are going to wear.

Conduct a search on the company to review their values, mission and vision, and align your image with what you believe the organisation's culture is like. You will want to 'bring yourself' to the interview, but it is helpful to understand the type of organisation they are, e.g., are they traditional or contemporary? Also, be clear about the expectations of the position you are applying for and do some research to find out how others in the same role are typically dressed.

You can and should bring your personality forward by electing one bold item.

An important reminder here is that they want to see your values, so it is best that you don't bring attention to anything in particular. Apply soft make up, one that enhances your traits, but does not overwhelm. This is not the time for shimmer or glitter! And avoid noisy jewellery, such as heavy bangles and large earrings. If you dress appropriately, they will see the value in the person and not pay attention to the dress.

Sharp tailoring with feminine details conveys a pleasant approachable result.

A shopping list and some tips for novices

You have probably heard the saying: Don't go grocery shopping when you are hungry. The same principle applies to shopping for clothes. Never go shopping when you are 'emotionally' hungry. That means, when you feel sad and want to comfort yourself, or when you are excited and want to reward yourself. At these times you run the risk of buying a beautiful top that won't go with anything in your wardrobe. Good planning should be practiced at all times when it comes to our closets. After all, we plan everything else, so why leave out what we will be adding to our wardrobe … our image?

Of course, we can reward ourselves every now and then, but avoid buying impulsively, so you don't collect clothing that you will never wear or may only wear once. And keep in mind that when we have a compact wardrobe and know its contents shopping becomes a breeze, because you have a clear idea of what piece you may be looking for and how it will go with what you already have.

Also, know how much you can afford. It is worth knowing what you have in your bank account to spare, as well as what you actually need in your closet. Also, take into consideration that winter items are usually more expensive than summer items.

Shop alone. Never go shopping with a friend, unless they can offer an honest opinion. Shopping is not like going to a party. Avoid a financial hangover the next morning!

Dress comfortably. Wear comfortable clothes when you shop, as you will be spending a lot of time in the fitting room. Also take the shoes you will wear your outfits with along with you.

Stay focused. If you intend to buy a pair of shoes, do not come home with a new bag!

Know what works for you. Listening to a second opinion is good, but at the end of the day, you are the one who will pay for and wear the item. If you are certain of what works for you, you will make the right decision when you look in the mirror. Remember it is your best friend and it never lies!

Always aim for the perfect ratio. Balance the types of clothes in your wardrobe. As I suggested, trendy pieces are ok as long as they don't make up the bulk of your wardrobe.

Listen to the emotion but use the reason. If you loved that sequin dress or those sky-high heels, really consider how many times you will wear them. Think about your lifestyle and routine. If you spend most of your days dropping kids off and picking them up, etc., you have to be realistic about what you are buying and how often you will actually wear it.

Buy to wear today – many of us fall into the trap of buying something we love, thinking about the diet you intend to do one day or the occasion that might come up. The item is likely to never see the light of day and, worse, the money wasted will never come back into your pocket!

Visualise mixing and matching. Since you can't bring your entire wardrobe with you, visualise how the items you're getting are going to work with what you already have at home. If you are getting a skirt, think about at least 3 tops that you can wear it with.

Check out the accessories. The jewellery section might be less intimidating to look at because it is usually in one small area. Try and have an open mind as you look through the pieces. Be creative. A necklace can be used as a headpiece, rings can be transformed into pendants and add sparkles to scarves, and pins can be worn on blazers, hats, and purses.

Wash the clothes before using them – once you get home from shopping, throw everything in the laundry right away but don't forget to read the tag for the recommended washing method before you do it.

Multiply

$$4 + 4 + 4 = 40$$

The beauty of understanding how to style pieces is that they multiply right before your eyes. Classic neutral pieces in colours such as black, navy, brown, beige, grey, and burgundy, are the foundation of your closet and they almost 'disappear' when you highlight more trendy items. Thus, people won't notice them if you wear them over and over. If you do it in a clever way you can create forty complete outfits from twelve pieces. So, for instance, four tops, fours bottoms, and four coats or jackets when combined will result in forty outfits. It is almost two months' worth of outfits! That illustrates how little we actually need to build a working wardrobe, or any wardrobe for that matter. How does that work?

Let's say you have four shirts, four jackets or coats, and four bottoms (skirts and pants). If they have neutral colours and a classic style to them, you can combine the pieces in a different manner every day for up to forty workdays!

Also think about dressing up and down a white shirt, wide leg pants, or that little black dress throughout the seasons. The key to creating good results is to remember proportions that compliment you as well as reinvigorate your style. A shirt on top of a strapless dress can make shoulders appear wider. If this is not your goal, finish off with a sleeveless vest instead. A ladylike dress looks less formal when paired with male-style loafers or sneakers. Have fun and experiment and remember that you can never go wrong with classics.

Packing for a business trip

Learning how to pack light luggage for a business trip will save you stress and money. First of all, design how your trip will be like. Check the local weather forecast and what you intend to do, i.e., business and tourism or only business. Consider who you are going to meet with. That will determine how formal or relaxed the pieces are going to be. Consider how much walking you are going to do, how many cocktail parties you will attend, or whether you are going to a gym, the beach, pool site, etc.

Tips:

- Wear your heavy pieces on board so you don't need to pack them.
- Bet on neutral colours, that way they will go with each other more easily.
- Bring some accessories, such as scarves, necklaces and belts to change up your outfit. Accessories do not take up much space.
- Do not overdo your toiletries. Take the minimum and use travel-sized bottles. Favour nude make-up colours. Bring only one little bottle of perfume.
- Refrain from bringing too many statement jewellery pieces. Opt for delicate, classic pieces.
- There is no need to bring one underwear per day as they can be washed and dried overnight.

- Bring a large carry-on bag and insert an evening purse in it in case you have an evening event.

  3-day/2-night trip plan:
- 1 raincoat/coat
- 1 pair of pants and 1 pair of jeans to travel back home
- 1 dress
- 1 skirt
- 2 shirt/blouse
- 1 t-shirt
- 1 pair of flat shoes/comfortable shoes
- 1 pair of mid-heels

  Double the tops and add one bottom if staying for a week.

  If you forget anything, you can always buy locally.

Beauty

In the Medicine Cabinet

As a stylist, I have worked with incredibly talented make-up artists, hairstylists and beauty gurus. So, what would a book about style be without talking about beauty? After all, there is no point in looking great from the neck down if you don't look as good from the neck up! Although, I should say that the older I get, the more I have started to invest in skincare as opposed to make-up. During my years in fashion, I saw make-up artists spending more time prepping the model's skin than applying their make-up. I heard many of them saying that make-up is as good as the quality of the skin, but I won't get into skincare here. Make-up is important, but it is just as important to adopt an uncomplicated skincare routine that enhances our faces. It's fundamental to composing a great complete look. Having said that, it is easy to get lost in the ocean of products available, so in this chapter, I'll try to guide you to your new findings.

"Seasonal makeup trends present a modern vision of beauty that inspires and shapes how we see ourselves. You don't have to wear every new style that comes down the runways but keeping current with what is 'now' tells the world that you're modern and open to new possibilities. Plus, an awareness of the latest trends gives you the freedom to adapt them to your personal style for a tailor-made approach to beauty." ~ Pat McGrath

There is no need to spend a fortune. Fortunately, there are many drugstore brands that are very good. To our advantage, there are fewer beauty trends in comparison to fashion ones.

When we are aware of what's current and know how to apply it, it only enhances the entire look. But not paying attention to these details can totally break an outfit.

So, where to spend?

It isn't that complicated! Women have a natural tendency to like everything beauty, especially make-up. Who hasn't played dressing up and practiced with their mom's red lipstick, right?

102

What is imperative is that a 'no make-up look' is what we are after here so that it almost looks like it is our skin, only enhanced. This look is timeless and will suit most occasions.

To achieve a look that goes well with what you wear, you need a few products and master a bit of technique that will save time. If there were one trick to learn about make-up, it would be *blending*. I cannot stress enough how crucial it is. And it is not hard to learn. It only takes patience and a bit of practice. Blend, blend and if in doubt, blend some more until you cannot see the beginning and the end of the product, whether it is eye shadow, blush or foundation.

When it comes to colours, it can be overwhelming, given the number of options that exist, so it is important to keep it simple. I would suggest choosing neutrals like light browns and taupes, preferably matte (particularly for day wear).

We all love luxurious beauty products like Chanel's gorgeous nail polishes or Dior's diva-like eyeshadows. But for the most part, we are just paying for the packaging. Did you know that huge cosmetic corporations own most beauty lines? For instance, Procter & Gamble own Frederic Fekkai, as well as Herbal Essences, Pantene, and Aussie Hair Care. L'Oréal oversees Lancôme, Shue Uemura, and Giorgio Armani. The giant Japanese brand Shiseido owns the luxurious brands Cle de Peau, Laura Mercier, Nars, and has recently acquired Dolce & Gabbana Beauty, as mentioned by Hillary Kerr and Katherine Power in their book *Who What Wear*.

It is important to know these facts, because we love the idea of spending on luxury items. The truth is these companies use pretty much the same technology and formulas on their products. Another interesting fact is that these companies hire celebrity make-up artists as their creative directors, who use their expertise to help develop products.

So, again, where to save and where to splurge?

Foundation:

When it comes to products applied on your face, such as foundation, powder, concealer, or BB or CC cream, it's best to invest in high-quality products that match your skin colour and type. Again, these are the two most important things to know about foundation: colour and purpose. Today, more and more brands are offering between 50 to 60 different shades, which makes finding your perfect colour a breeze. There are lots of hybrid options that serve as skincare/make-up. But this is completely optional.

Brushes:

Good-quality brushes are very important, as they provide a more even and light application, delivering accuracy with minimal strokes, which also helps save time. You can also opt for a beauty sponge for a lighter, dewier coverage.

Eye Shadow:

Along the same lines as foundation, high-end brand eyeshadows deliver more pigments and thus last longer. They also have more buildable, beautiful colours.

Conditioner:

Investing in a good hair conditioner and styling products is a smart move. These products are supposed to treat and protect hair from environmental aggressors and the heating tools we put our hair in contact with on a regular basis. Opt for quality products.

Hot tools: The technology used in pricier products makes them well worth their price, as they heat up evenly and faster. This is crucial for achieving a great result.

Where to save?

Mascaras: When it comes to innovation, mascaras are at the forefront. There are fibre formulas, 3D-printed wands, bottom lashes mascaras, the list goes on. I've always heard from make-up artists that mascaras have the same formula, the only difference being the wand. Now I know that this is not true. Because mascaras don't have a long shelf life, there's no point in breaking the bank buying the expensive stuff. But again, the cheaper versions need a more precise application and can go gloopy much more often than the high-end ones. What differentiates them from one another is the wand and how you apply it. Technique is key when applying mascara. But the choice is yours. If you opt for more affordable versions, know that you will have to work harder to keep it from going gloopy; if you do opt for the expensive ones, they don't last for a long time anyway, so again it is a personal choice.

Lip gloss/lipstick: No gloss or lipstick will last long, so there is absolutely no need to spend a lot on these.

Shampoos: Shampoos are supposed to clean your hair, and that's it. Remember, the cosmetic industry will encourage you to buy as much as they can by launching 'high tech,' 'out of this world' products, such as scalp scrubs and the like, but the bottom line is you can as easily use home-made formulas for the same result. A great one is lemon juice and sugar. I use that all over my body; just be careful to not get sun exposure as the lemon acids will damage your skin.

Classic looks: If you ever have to choose just one eyeshadow colour, make it brown as it compliments all eye colours.

Red lips: Sleek, glamorous or 'French girl.' This is a classic that has to be mastered to enhance your look. Make sure you exfoliate your lips for a more uniform application, and always use a pencil to contour the lips and prevent colour bleeding. As a rule of thumb, when putting on a bright pout, keep the eyes neutral. A light beige shadow and mascara will do the trick. Also remember that red lips are high maintenance, so keep your lipstick in your purse for touch-ups. On a lower maintenance level, try a stain. Because they are more sheer than a regular lipstick, you don't need to worry about contouring the lips or reapplying. But no red is for everybody; if you are warm, opt for orange-reds, and if you are cool, try the purple-red colours.

Romantic: Rosy tones are always pretty and complimentary to most skin tones. It is a great option for a first date or a day wedding.

Job interview: For a job interview as well as the office, it is important that you wear make-up. Do not attempt to go bare faced. Take the less is more approach and wear little foundation, or simply a BB/CC cream to even out your skin tone. Light eyeshadow, mascara and a nude lipstick are pretty much all you need to look polished and professional. Avoid shimmer eyeshadows, or too much contouring and highlight. Leave those for special occasions. Matte colours are more appropriate. The idea is to enhance the skin without looking too made up.

Formal occasions: Now you can create a more elaborate look by marking the corner of the eye with darker shades and adding a bit of shimmer on the eyelid. Avoid shimmer above the eyelid, especially if you are older than twenty. Adding eyeliner shapes the eyes and can make them appear larger. If you want the opposite effect, line the rim of the eye.

Conclusion

The more time I spend with women, the more I realise how important it is to have a well-planned, organised, de-cluttered wardrobe. We are more and more pressed for time and our daily routines only get busier as we advance our careers and have children.

It all starts with all the excitement of entering the work force and realising how tough it actually is. We are competing against male counterparts who clearly have an advantage. Then later on we face the challenges of having a family and juggling between parenting and work. Growing kids will demand more of our time as they start becoming more active. We can end up forgetting about ourselves, losing identity, and facing life and bodily changes all at the same time. With that comes a lack of confidence and the feeling of guilt when we decide to think of ourselves.

But even if having a family didn't happen for you, for whatever reason, know that this book is also for you. I want this book to be inclusive rather than exclusive and reach women from all paths of life. More and more women are leaving motherhood for later or choosing to not have children or even get married at all. So, their career becomes their main focus. The pressure and expectation of success can take a big toll on us. And for some, our efforts are not always valued, and we often make less money and are offered lower positions in tough economic periods. As we are all aware, the world is not yet a fair place.

My passion is to attempt to relieve some of this burden by bringing awareness to the *here and now.* To help us accept where we are at the present moment and not lose track. In practical terms this means recognising what makes us look our best, de-cluttering our wardrobes of what no longer suits us, and planning a wardrobe that will reflect this new you. It also includes having an uncomplicated beauty routine with the right products that will enhance your natural beauty. You deserve that! This will give you a stress-free morning, when all you need to do is open your closet and know where everything is. Best of all, if you have pieces that go with each other and suit you perfectly, you don't need to waste time thinking about what you are going to wear and trying on things at the last minute. You should not have to compromise on the result because you are pressed for time. Being in the present moment and not losing track will always result in you looking your best despite what life is bringing you.

I also want you to have a more pleasant shopping experience, where you shop with purpose and some planning. Shopping to reward or comfort ourselves is fine when it is a one-off event but making this a habit only contributes to cluttering our wardrobes and our minds, not to mention the hole it leaves in our wallets.

I hope the ideas I mentioned in this book can help you in some small way to improve your image and how you and others perceive you and simplify your life while bringing renewed confidence in your ability to achieve your life goals, whatever they are. In closing, I would like to quote Yves Saint Laurent, one of the greatest designers of all time, as this quote sums up everything this book is about:

"Finding your own style is not easy, but once found it brings happiness. It gives you self-confidence, always."
~ Yves Saint Laurent

Appendix

Online shops:

The Outnet.com

Zara

H&M

Topshop.co.uk

Mango.com

Asos.com

Net-a-porter.com

Matchesfashion.com

Luisaviaroma.com

Shopstyle.com

Shopbop.com

Urbanoutfitters.com

Farfetch.com

Modaoperandi.com

Mytheresa.com

Forzieri.com

Yoox.com

Online Resale shops:

Therealreal.com

Ebay.com

Nastygalvintage.com

VestiareCollective.com

References

Adam, H., & Galinsky, A.D. (2012). Enclothed cognition. Journal of Experimental Social Psychology, 48(4), 918-925.

Eiserman, L. & Cutler, E.P. (2014). Pantone on Fashion: A Century of Colour in Design. Chronicle Books, San Francisco.

Kerr, H. and Power, K. (2009). Who, What, Wear. Abrams Image: New York: NY.

Khalil Gloria - Chic, Um guia de moda e estilo para o século XXI, Editora Senac

Kurt, S. & Kingsley Osueke, K. (2014). The effects of colour on the moods of college students. SAGE Open (Jan-Mar), pp. 1.-12.

Kraus, M. W., & Mendes, W. B. (2014). Sartorial symbols of social class elicit class-consistent behavioural and physiological responses: A dyadic approach. *Journal of Experimental Psychology: General, 143*(6), 2330-2340. http://dx.doi.org/10.1037/xge0000023

Morris, T. (2011). Feng shui your life. Turner Publishing Company., Nashville, Tennessee.

Rasband Judith (2002). Wardrobe Strategies for Women. Fairchild Publications Inc., New York.

Rees, A. (2014). How to assess the quality of garments: A beginner's guide part 1. May 2014. https://anuschkarees. com/blog/2014/05/01/how-to-assess-the-quality-of-garments-a-beginners-guide-part-i

Slepian, M.L., Ferber, S.N., Gold, J.M. & Rutchick, A.M. (2015). The cognitive consequences of formal clothing. Social Psychological and Personality Science, 6(6).

Printed in Great Britain
by Amazon

36927233R00075